Native
American
Peoples

CHEROKEE

D. L. Birchfield

Gareth Stevens Publishing

A WORLD ALMANAC EDUCATION GROUP COMPANY

Please visit our web site at: www.garethstevens.com
For a free color catalog describing Gareth Stevens Publishing's list of high-quality books
and multimedia programs, call 1-800-542-2595 (USA) or 1-800-387-3178 (Canada).
Gareth Stevens Publishing's fax: (414) 332-3567.

Library of Congress Cataloging-in-Publication Data

Birchfield, D. L., 1948-
    Cherokee / by D. L. Birchfield.
      p. cm. — (Native American peoples)
    Summary: Examines the history, art, language, culture, and future prospects of the
Cherokee Indians, as well as distinguished members of the tribe.
    Includes bibliographical references and index.
    ISBN 0-8368-3700-2 (lib. bdg.)
    1. Cherokee Indians—Juvenile literature. [1. Cherokee Indians. 2. Indians of
North America—Oklahoma. 3. Indians of North America—Southern States.]
    I. Title. II. Series.
    E99.C5B482 2003
    975.004'9755—dc21
                                       2003045706

First published in 2004 by
Gareth Stevens Publishing
A World Almanac Education Group Company
330 West Olive Street, Suite 100
Milwaukee, WI 53212 USA

Copyright © 2004 by Gareth Stevens Publishing.

Produced by Discovery Books
Project editor: Valerie J. Weber
Designer and page production: Sabine Beaupré
Photo researcher: Rachel Tisdale
Native American consultant: Robert J. Conley, M.A., Former Director of Native American
  Studies at Morningside College and Montana State University
Maps and diagrams: Stefan Chabluk
Gareth Stevens editorial direction: Mark Sachner
Gareth Stevens art direction: Tammy Gruenewald
Gareth Stevens production: Beth Meinholz and Jessica L. Yanke

Photo credits: Native Stock: cover, pp. 5, 8 (top), 12 (top), 14, 15, 16, 17 (both), 19 (both), 21,
24, 25, 27 (top); Corbis: pp. 13, 18, 20, 23, 27; North Wind Picture Archives: pp. 6, 8 (bottom);
Peter Newark's American Pictures: pp. 7, 9, 10, 11, 12 (bottom), 22.

Printed in the United States of America

1 2 3 4 5 6 7 8 9 07 06 05 04 03

Cover caption: A Cherokee man in a traditional powwow outfit. Today, many powwows
include dancers competing for prizes.

Contents

Words that appear in the glossary are printed in **boldface** type the first time they appear in the text.

Origins

The Cherokees' homeland once included a large area of today's southeastern United States. Most Cherokee villages were in the southern Appalachian Mountains of present-day North Carolina, Georgia, and Tennessee.

Cherokee Country

The Cherokees are a North American Native people whose homelands in the southern Appalachian Mountains once included parts of present-day Kentucky, West Virginia, Virginia, North Carolina, South Carolina, Georgia, Alabama, and Tennessee. They are by far the largest Native **nation** in the United States, with a total tribal membership close to 275,000 people. Many Cherokees are mixed bloods — part Indian, part non-Indian — due to their long history of **intermarriage** with whites.

Today, about ten thousand Eastern Cherokees live on or near the Qualla Boundary **reservation** in North Carolina, but most Cherokees live in the Cherokee Nation in northeastern Oklahoma. Many thousands also live throughout the United States and Canada.

Cherokee Origins

Cherokee origin stories tell of a time when water covered the earth. Land was formed when a water beetle dove deep into the ocean and scooped up mud, bringing it to the surface to make the earth.

Home of Cherokees for centuries, the southern Appalachian Mountains in North Carolina are a place of great natural beauty. Today, the Great Smoky Mountains National Park is located near the reservation of the Eastern Band Cherokee Indians.

No one knows for sure how long Cherokees and other Indians might have been in North America, how they got here, or from where they came. Many scholars believe, however, that Indians may have crossed a landmass stretching over the Bering Strait between North America and Asia during the latest Ice Age. Recent discoveries, however, have pushed the dates of Indian presence in North America further back in time than the Ice Age.

The name *Cherokee* (or *Tsa-la-gi)* is thought to be a Choctaw word meaning "cave people." The Cherokees' name for themselves is *Ani-yun-wiya,* meaning the "real people" or "original people."

Cherokee Words

Cherokee is an **Iroquoian** language that is distantly related to the language of the Mohawks and other Iroquoian tribes in the Northeast. Some scholars estimate that it has been developing separately for about thirty-five hundred years.

Cherokee	Pronunciation	English
asgaya	ahs-kay-ya	man
agehya	ah-gay-hyuh	woman
sogwili	so-gwee-lee	horse
osiyo	oh-see-yo	hello
awi	ah-whee	deer
saloli	sa-lo-li	squirrel
galijodii	gahl-jo-dee	house

History

The Europeans Arrive

Before Europeans came to North America, Cherokees were farmers living in villages in Appalachian Mountain valleys. They harvested large crops of corn, beans, and squash and gathered nuts, berries, wild onions, and other food in the forest. Hunting provided meat.

By the early 1600s, the English had established colonies along the Atlantic coast. Settlers soon began taking over Cherokee land in Virginia, forcing some villages to relocate farther inland in the Appalachian Mountains, where most Cherokees lived. By the 1670s, Cherokees were trading with the English, exchanging deerskins and animal furs for metal pots, knives, axes, and other useful things. Before long, they began trading for guns, which they soon became dependent upon.

Power Provides Little Protection

By 1729, about twenty thousand Cherokees lived in about sixty-four towns. Though a powerful nation, the Cherokees were not

Made in the 1660s, this painting shows the Indian village of Secotan in North Carolina. At that time, North Carolina was part of Virginia Colony.

able to avoid the wars that Europeans fought with one another in North America, and European armies sometimes burned Indian villages during their own battles.

This portrait was drawn of three Cherokee chiefs in 1762, when they were visiting London, England.

As the United States became independent from England in 1783, the country's desire for land — even that belonging to the Cherokees — grew. Settlers flocked into Cherokee country, including present-day Georgia. When the new nation acquired land west of the Mississippi River in the Louisiana Purchase in 1803, President Thomas Jefferson decided that all the eastern Indian nations would have to give up their own land and move west. The federal government would remove the Indians; Georgia's government agreed.

President Jefferson's Indian Policy

President Thomas Jefferson played a big role in the Cherokees' losing their land. In 1803, Jefferson began a scheme to give the Indians unlimited **credit** at government-owned trading posts, hoping they would go deeply into debt buying trade goods. They would then have to trade their land to the government to pay their bills. That's exactly what happened; each U.S. **treaty** with the Cherokees required them to give up more land. Thus, the United States acquired millions of acres of land very cheaply.

The first Native American-language newspaper, the *Cherokee Phoenix*, in 1828. It used the set of written Cherokee characters invented by Sequoyah.

A Time of Change

The Cherokees realized they could lose their ancient homeland and tried to avoid removal by embracing many white practices, hoping the whites would then consider them as equals. They adopted a written **constitution** and laws, forming a government modeled on that of the United States. They changed the way they dressed and began looking like the white settlers. They also invited **missionaries** into the nation, who started schools and churches.

Perhaps most remarkably, a Cherokee named Sequoyah invented a way of writing the Cherokee language that could be learned quickly and easily. The Natives soon learned how to read and write their language and began publishing their own newspaper, the *Cherokee Phoenix,* in both English and Cherokee.

This painting shows gold miners in the Cherokee country in present-day Georgia in the late 1820s. The "Southern Gold Rush" on Cherokee land caused many Americans, especially Georgians, to demand Cherokee removal.

Land in Danger

Nothing the Cherokees did, however, satisfied the people of Georgia, who wanted Indian land. In 1828, General Andrew Jackson was elected president, promising to remove the Indians from the South. In 1829, gold was discovered in the southern part of the Cherokee Nation, and a wild gold rush started. Miners stole the Cherokee gold and demanded the Indians give up their land.

In 1830, Congress passed the Indian Removal Act. The Cherokees also began to use the legal system to protect their rights, however, winning an important decision from the U.S. Supreme Court. This 1832 case made clear that Georgia could not extend its laws into the Cherokee Nation and that the tribe was an independent nation. The Cherokees gained the respect and sympathy of many Americans, who protested Georgia's demand that the Natives move.

In 1835, ignoring the 1832 Supreme Court decision, President Jackson pressured a small **minority** of Cherokees — who were not elected by their people — into signing a removal treaty. These Cherokees quickly moved to the West, but the great majority of the tribe, under Chief John Ross, refused to leave. They clung to the hope that they would not be forced to forsake their ancient homeland.

Son of a Scottish father and an Indian mother, Chief John Ross led his people on the forced march to Indian Territory from 1838 to 1839.

It is no doubt good policy in the states to get rid of all the Indians within their limits as soon as possible; [but] in doing so, they care very little where they send them, provided they get them out of the limits of their state. . . . This we consider the worst policy our government can pursue with the Indians.

Arkansas Gazette, *1829, Arkansas Territory*

U.S. Army General Winfield Scott was in charge of the Cherokee removal. He became a war hero during the Mexican-American War of 1846 to 1848.

Men working in the fields were arrested and driven to the **stockades**. Women were dragged from their homes by soldiers whose language they could not understand. Children were often separated from their parents and driven into the stockades. . . . And often the old and the infirm were prodded with bayonets to hasten them to the stockade.

U.S. Army Private John G. Burnett, who participated in the Cherokee removal of 1838

The Trail of Tears

Cherokee removal came suddenly. In 1838, General Winfield Scott invaded the Cherokee country with seven thousand U.S. Army soldiers and Georgia volunteers. They swept through the countryside, rounding up Cherokee families by the thousands and herding them into prison camps. Hundreds of Cherokees died there from disease.

During the winter of 1838 to 1839, the U.S. Army divided the Cherokees into thirteen groups of about one thousand each and started them west. Many had to walk barefoot on the frozen ground, without enough food and with only one blanket per person for shelter from the cold. The Cherokees traveled about 800 miles (1,300 kilometers) to present-day northeastern Oklahoma, leaving their dead along the way. Their terrible journey became known as the Trail of Tears.

The removal killed about four thousand Cherokees, but many more died of illness after arriving in the West. The Cherokee removal was one of the cruelest episodes in U.S. history.

Left Behind

When the great majority of Cherokees were removed in the 1830s, several hundred tribal members in North Carolina claimed they lived outside the Cherokee

No one painted the Cherokee removal of 1838 to 1839 at the time, but this later painting, by Robert Lindneux, is his interpretation of what the removal might have looked like.

Nation on land **ceded** to the United States in earlier treaties. Though their legal status was greatly in doubt, the U.S. Army did not attempt to remove them.

Life in the New Land

Forced to leave their homeland, some Cherokees turned on the small minority of Cherokees who had signed the treaty. In 1839, some of those signers were killed, and the nation was thrown into unrest.

It was seven years before the Cherokees living in the West finally made an uneasy peace among themselves and began rebuilding their lives. Under Chief John Ross,

I fought through the civil war and have seen men shot to pieces and slaughtered by thousands, but the Cherokee removal was the cruelest work I ever knew.

A Confederate Civil War colonel who had participated in the Cherokee removal in 1838 as a Georgia volunteer

This painting, by John Mix Stanley, depicts a gathering of seventeen Indian nations in 1843 in Tahlequah in the Cherokee Nation. The Cherokees sponsored this meeting to discuss common problems.

The *Cherokee Primer*, 1845. This small book was used by children in the Cherokee Nation public school system. By the late nineteenth century, the Cherokees had developed a school system that was better than that of most states in the region.

they created a Cherokee public school system and two colleges, called seminaries. They published the *Cherokee Advocate* newspaper and governed themselves under a written constitution, modeled somewhat on the U.S. Constitution, with officials elected in general elections.

Civil War Erupts

The U.S. government had promised in treaties to protect the Cherokees, but when the **Civil War** broke out in 1861, the government withdrew all its troops in their lands, leaving the Indians helpless. Many had to flee from their homes as armies from both sides swept through their land, stealing all their food and animals and burning almost all the buildings. About one-fourth of the Cherokee people died during the war, mostly from starvation and disease in **refugee** camps.

Cherokees fought on both sides during the war, but the victorious North treated all Cherokees as defeated enemies at the

The U.S. Congress began forcing the Cherokees to give up their land in the late nineteenth century. The Cherokee Strip was opened up to whites in a land run in 1893; they raced one another to stake a claim to a farm.

war's end, forcing them to sign a harsh treaty in 1866. The treaty required them to give up land, allow the railroad to build in their nation, and put them under U.S. laws. After the war, whites swarmed onto the Cherokee Nation until they outnumbered the Indians and began demanding their land.

Dividing the Land and People

During the 1890s, Congress forced the Cherokees to divide the land held by the tribe as a whole and accept individual ownership of small farms; the government then sold the remaining Cherokee land to white settlers. In 1907, when the state of Oklahoma was created, the U.S. government claimed that the Cherokee Nation had been abolished.

For most of the twentieth century, the U.S. government tried to end the status of the Cherokees and other Indian groups as independent nations. Until the 1970s, in fact, Cherokee chiefs were appointed by the U.S. president, sometimes only for one day, just to have someone to sign legal papers.

A Promise Broken
The United States hereby . . . agree that the lands ceded to the Cherokee nation . . . [will never] be included within the territorial limits . . . of any State or Territory.

U.S. government's treaty with the Cherokees, 1835

Traditional Way of Life

A Farming People

The traditional Cherokee lifestyle was based on farming; hunting and fishing also provided food. Everyone helped with the town farm plots, and the resulting crops belonged to all. Each family also worked its own fields. Those farms, as well as the family houses, belonged to the women.

The Cherokees were expert farmers, growing mainly corn, beans, and squash, as well as many other crops, such as melons and tobacco. They also raised turkeys for food as well as hunting them in the wild. After Europeans introduced hogs, cattle, chickens, and horses, Cherokees soon reared these in large numbers, too.

Traditional Cherokee food is an important part of many Cherokee gatherings. Here, the feast includes pig back fat, mustard greens, chestnut bread, and butternut squash.

A Land of Plenty

Experts at harvesting the natural resources of their homeland, Cherokees gathered large crops of pecans and other nuts in the fall, wild onions in the spring, and the blackberries that grew thickly on the hillsides in the summer. Deer, elk, bears, mountain lions, and wolves filled their forests, while herds of buffaloes grazed on the famous "blue grass" prairies of their hunting grounds.

European trade goods brought great changes. To have deer hides and animal furs to trade, the Cherokee had to hunt the animals as they never had before — for money. Soon their prey became scarce; the hunters

Finely crafted Cherokee pottery was an important part of their trade goods as well as their home life.

couldn't gather enough hides and furs for trade. Before long, the Cherokees had little to trade except their land.

"Five Civilized Tribes"

European settlers called the Cherokees, along with the Choctaws, Chickasaws, Seminoles, and Muskogee/Creeks, the Five Civilized Tribes. The settlers were impressed when they saw these skilled farmers who lived mostly in their own large towns in highly organized societies. The Cherokees were also gifted public speakers and diplomats, quickly earning the respect of the Europeans who settled near them.

In a historical Cherokee village, built for tourists, visitors can see how a traditional Cherokee house was constructed.

Cherokee Towns

Cherokee villages were often built like forts, with a high stockade fence made of logs surrounding them. In the center of the village stood at least one large building for public meetings, other public buildings for storing corn, and ball fields for playing games. Cherokee homes, with walls of branches held together with mud, surrounded the central public area.

Each town had its own independent government. All the men and women were allowed to speak when discussing issues. Decisions were not by majority vote, but by **consensus**, meaning that most people finally reached agreement. Cherokees who did not agree with the consensus were free to ignore the decision, move to another village, or start a new village of their own.

Family Life

Children spent most of their time playing, often with a blowgun made by an older relative from a long piece of cane. Spending many hours hunting squirrels and rabbits in the woods near the village, they learned to shoot darts through the blowgun. When the children were older, they received a bow and arrows and learned to hunt larger game, such as deer. By the time they were teenagers, most young Cherokees were expert hunters.

Generally, women took care of the home, cooked, made clothing, and tended the agricultural fields, while men hunted, made weapons, and fought enemies in times of war. Women could also become warriors, however. Most women did not choose to do so, but some who did became famous, earning the respected name "War Woman."

In a reconstructed Cherokee village at the Cherokee Heritage Center in the Cherokee Nation near Tahlequah, a woman is showing how to grind corn into cornmeal.

Cherokee Clothing

Before European contact, traditional Cherokee summer clothing consisted of a breechcloth and moccasins for most men and a short skirt for women. In cold weather, women added a pull-over top, and men wore a hunting jacket and leggings. All were made of deerskin.

During the 1800s, men began wearing shirts and jackets made of cloth, and women began weaving blouses and long dresses. Some men also wore a turban around their head. By the late 1800s, many Cherokees dressed like the white people on the frontier.

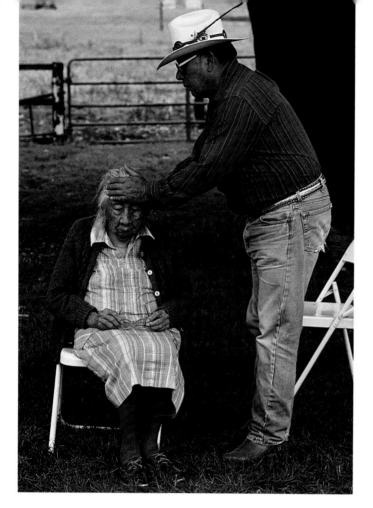

A woman visits a Cherokee **medicine man**. Today, many Cherokees still prefer to seek the knowledge that traditional doctors have learned from many centuries of traditional Cherokee medical practice.

Traditional Stories

Stories are an important part of Cherokee traditional life, teaching children about their history, traditions, culture, and the morals of the Cherokee belief system. For example, traditional stories explain the origin of illness and its treatment. According to one such traditional story, long ago, the animals held a council to discuss a problem: the people were killing too many animals without showing proper respect for the lives they were taking. Each animal created an illness that would punish the people.

When the plants heard what the animals were doing, they felt sorry for the people, and each plant created a cure for an illness. The story explains how the Cherokees had to learn to show respect for the lives of animals they took and to live in harmony with the animals and plants.

Traditional Games

Games have also formed a vital part of Cherokee traditional life. Stickball games, similar to the game of lacrosse, between Cherokee towns were by far the most important. All other

Cherokee women playing stickball. The game is an ancient part of Cherokee culture, and it remains important to all the southeastern Indian tribes and to many other tribes in North America.

activities came to a standstill when a stickball match was being played. Medicine men for both sides were employed to make charms that might bring victory in the game. Frequently, the people of the opposing towns bet everything of any value that they possessed on the outcome of the game. Today, stickball is often played both as a game and as an important part of rituals at ceremonial grounds.

Stickball Games

The favorite time is in the fall, after the corn has ripened . . . at this season a game takes place somewhere on the reservation at least every other week . . . but the exact spot selected [for the game] is always a matter of uncertainty up to the last moment. . . . If this were not the case, a spy from the other settlement might [try] to insure the defeat of the party by strewing along their trail a soup made of the hamstrings of rabbits, which would have the effect of rendering the players [timid] and easily confused.

James Mooney, a scholar and author, in 1890

Stickball sticks were made of hickory, with a webbed pocket made of leather. The ball was originally made of deerskin.

19

Beliefs

In Cherokee traditional culture, the world was described as being like a giant bowl turned upside down on a saucer, forming a big dome. The earth is underneath the dome, floating on water. The sky fills the dome all the way to the underside of the bowl, which is called the Sky Vault. The Sun travels across the sky each day just beneath the Sky Vault, which is made of rock. At the end of its journey, it slips underneath the Sky Vault so it can return to its starting point and cross the sky again the next day.

This mask is used for a traditional Cherokee dance called the Booger Dance. Dances have always been important community activities for Cherokees, a time of feasting and visiting.

On top of the Sky Vault is another world, very much like the earth. The souls of departed Cherokees live there, along with spirit beings.

Another world also exists underneath the earth, but it is just the opposite of life on the earth. When it is daytime on the earth, it is nighttime there. When it is summer on the earth, it is winter there. This underworld is home for many powerful, dangerous spirit forces.

The worlds above and below the earth represent extremes. Traditional Cherokees believe that they live their lives between those two extremes, constantly trying to maintain harmony and balance between the two. Most Cherokee rituals, ceremonies, and the old habits of living are intended to help maintain that balance and harmony.

Stomp Dance

The Cherokee Stomp Dance is a sacred dance, ordinarily held at Stomp Grounds in the countryside. Each of the Grounds has its own religious leaders. Their locations are unknown to non-Cherokees; they are not for tourists. The Stomp Dance is performed in a counter-clockwise direction around a sacred fire. Participants engage in this and other dances and ceremonies all night long, once a month between spring and fall. Occasionally, the Stomp Dance is also performed at other cultural events as a way of teaching others about traditional Cherokee life.

Children being taught the Cherokee Stomp Dance. These dances are very popular today. Some are held in public; others take place at more remote Stomp Grounds in the countryside.

Today

Entertainer and humorist Will Rogers (1879–1935) became one of the best-known Cherokees in the world. He is shown here at his first vaudeville appearance in New York City in 1905.

Literature and Art

The Cherokees have produced many scholars, writers, playwrights, poets, actors, and artists. Some world-famous people, such as Oklahoma humorist Will Rogers, had Cherokee blood.

Lynn Riggs wrote a play called *Green Grow the Lilacs*, which was later converted into a musical by Richard Rodgers and Oscar Hammerstein. This became one of the most famous Broadway plays of all time — *Oklahoma!*

Poet Geary Hobson, author of *Deer Hunting and Other Poems*, is a professor of English at the University of Oklahoma. He edited one of the most important collections of American Indian literature, *The Remembered Earth*.

Rennard Strickland has become one of the foremost scholars on Indian law. Now dean of the law school at the University of Oregon, he was president of the American Association of Law Schools in 1994.

A number of Cherokees are currently working with materials from their traditional culture. Artist Murv Jacob paints pictures of traditional life, many of which hang on the walls of the Cherokee Nation headquarters in Tahlequah, Oklahoma. An acclaimed author of children's books about Cherokee life, storyteller Gail

Ross has entertained thousands of people with traditional tales. Novelist Robert J. Conley brings alive the oldest Cherokee stories about their history in his Real People series. He has received the Cherokee Medal of Honor from the Cherokee Honor Society and is now in the Oklahoma Professional Writers Hall of Fame. An international opera star, Barbara McAlister sometimes sings an ancient lullaby, one of the oldest surviving Cherokee songs, in her performances.

Wes Studi

Famous for his Hollywood movies, Oklahoma Cherokee actor Wes Studi starred in *Geronimo: An American Legend.* He also played the unforgettable role of Magua in *Last of the Mohicans.* He keeps in close contact with his people and attended the inauguration of the new Cherokee chief, Chad Smith, at the Cherokee capitol in August 2000.

Cherokee actor Wes Studi, as he appeared in the movie *Geronimo: An American Legend.* Wes Studi has become one of the busiest and best-known American Indian actors in Hollywood.

The Eastern Cherokees

In the mid-nineteenth century, William Thomas, a white man raised by Eastern Cherokees, bought land for them at the edge of the mountains, property that later became known as the Qualla Boundary. After the Civil War, others joined the Eastern Cherokees on their reservation in North Carolina.

During the twentieth century, tourism became the most important part of the Eastern Cherokees' **economy**, especially after 1940 when the Great Smoky Mountains National Park opened next to the reservation. Today, they have added **casinos** to their economy, and millions of tourists visit the reservation each year.

By the early twenty-first century, the Eastern Band owned more than 56,000 acres (22,700 hectares) of land. Their population is now more than ten thousand. Eastern Cherokees

Cherokee women compete in a blowgun contest. With practice, the blowgun can be used with great accuracy.

Like children everywhere, Cherokee schoolchildren love recess. This school is located on the Qualla Boundary reservation in North Carolina.

today have little opportunity for continuing their centuries-old skills as farmers except for raising family vegetable gardens. Most of their reservation is now mountain land thickly covered with trees.

The Western Cherokees

Today, two Cherokee tribes now lie within the boundaries of the Cherokee Nation in the West — the United Keetoowah Band of Cherokee Indians, Oklahoma, and the Cherokee Nation. Numbering ten thousand members, the Keetoowah Band is much smaller and older than the Cherokee Nation.

Both the Keetoowah Band and the Cherokee Nation have their tribal headquarters in Tahlequah, Oklahoma, the historic capitol of the Cherokees in the West. The Cherokee Nation, with over 240,000, is not only the largest Cherokee tribe but also the largest

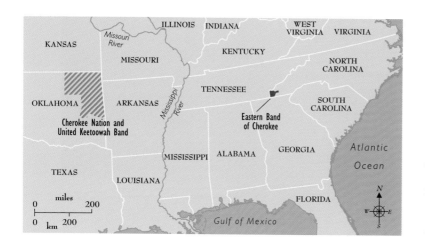

The Cherokee Nation today includes the same land as the old Cherokee Nation did in Indian Territory. The Cherokee Nation and the State of Oklahoma both claim the same land.

Indian nation in the United States by far. It was reorganized in the 1970s. The Cherokee Nation gained federal recognition under a new constitution when the U.S. government gave up its 1907 claim that Indian tribes in Oklahoma had been abolished when that territory became a state.

A Nation Renewed

As the U.S. government changed its policy toward Native American governments and upheld laws to allow them to govern themselves, the Cherokee Nation became a leader among Indian tribes. It now manages many tribal programs, ranging from educational programs for Cherokee children to housing programs, that were once run by the U.S. government. This has helped make the Cherokee Nation a large employer in the region, a multimillion-dollar enterprise with a great impact on the local economy.

Today, Cherokee Nation children in northeastern Oklahoma again have an opportunity to learn from Cherokee teachers. Many state public schools in the Nation have Cherokee cultural programs funded by the U.S. government, and many also have Head Start programs, which offer early learning opportunities, for preschoolers. The Cherokee Nation now operates Sequoyah High School, which used to be a boarding school run by the U.S. government, in Tahlequah.

Many young Cherokees stay at home to go to college. Northeastern Oklahoma State University, in Tahlequah, has the highest enrollment of Indian college students of any university in the United States, more than one thousand Indian students each semester. Many of those college students become schoolteachers in the Oklahoma public school system.

The Cherokee Nation headquarters building near Tahlequah. The Cherokee Nation tribal complex has many buildings, including a restaurant and gift shop.

The Cherokee people, both Eastern and Western, are entering the twenty-first century with renewed hope for the future. They are once again governing themselves and are seeking more self-determination for their futures.

Wilma Mankiller

Wilma Mankiller and President Reagan (left) in a 1988 meeting at White House.

Wilma Mankiller (born 1945) gained international recognition as a political leader as the first female principal chief of the Cherokee Nation from 1985 to 1994. During that time, she guided her people into the modern era by helping it gain the right to self-government and also brought needed programs and services to the tribe. In 1998, she received the Congressional Medal of Freedom from President Bill Clinton. A leader among Natives and non-Natives alike, she still speaks publicly on issues of concern to Indians and women.

Time Line

1776	American Revolution; most Cherokees side with the English.
1785	Cherokees agree to first treaty with the United States.
1803	U.S. government outlaws Indians owning land within Georgia, urges Eastern tribes to move west.
1817	In U.S. treaty, Cherokees trade for some land in West; some Cherokee "old settlers" volunteer to move there.
1821	Sequoyah invents a system of writing the Cherokee language.
1827	The Cherokee Nation adopts constitution; elect John Ross chief.
1828	First Indian language newspaper, *Cherokee Phoenix,* is founded.
1829	Georgians discover gold on Cherokee land; Georgia legislature tries to extend state laws over Cherokees.
1835	Small number of Cherokees sign treaty agreeing to move.
1838–39	General Winfield Scott's large U.S. Army invades Cherokee homeland; Cherokee Trail of Tears; thousands die.
1840s	Cherokees rebuild their lives in the West, adopt new Cherokee constitution, and establish *Cherokee Advocate.*
1861–65	U.S. Civil War devastates Cherokee land.
1887	Congress passes law to divide tribal lands; remaining land sold to white settlers.
1889	Eastern Cherokee reservation established in North Carolina.
1907	Government claims Cherokee Nation no longer exists.
1900s	U.S. presidents appoint Cherokee chiefs because federal government needs someone to sign legal papers occasionally.
late 1960s– early '70s	Violent Indian protests bring world attention to U.S. U.S. government allows Cherokees to adopt new constitutions and form tribal governments again.
1983	Cherokees elect Wilma Mankiller principal chief.
1990	Cherokees take control of many federal Cherokee programs.

Glossary

casinos: buildings that have slot machines, card games, and other gambling games.

ceded: gave up ownership of something.

Civil War: the war between northern and southern U.S. states that lasted from 1861 to 1865.

consensus: an agreement among all individuals in a group to an opinion or position.

constitution: the basic laws and principles of a nation that outline the powers of the government and the rights of the people.

credit: the ability to make purchases without paying money for the items immediately.

economy: the way a country or people produces, divides up, and uses its goods and money.

intermarriage: a term used to describe marriages between members of different groups.

Iroquoian: describes a large family of Indian languages, mostly in eastern North America, which includes those of the Cherokees and Mohawks.

medicine man: a religious leader and healer.

minority: the smaller in number of two groups forming a whole.

missionaries: people who try to teach others their religion.

nation: people who have their own customs, laws, and land separate from other nations or people.

refugee: a person who is forced to leave his or her home to find safety and protection.

reservation: land set aside by the U.S. government.

stockades: large prison camps surrounded by fences and guarded by soldiers.

treaty: an agreement among nations or people.

More Resources

Web Sites:

http://www.cherokee.org/Culture/Kids.asp The Kids Corner of the official web site of the Cherokee Nation has answers to frequently asked questions about Cherokee culture and history, kids' games, and traditional stories.

Videos:

500 Nations. Warner Home Video, 1995.

The War Against the Indians: The Dispossessed. Madarcy Records, *1995.*

Books:

Bial, Raymond. *The Cherokee* (Lifeways). Marshall Cavendish, 1999.

Birchfield, D. L. *The Trail of Tears* (Landmark Events in American History). Gareth Stevens, 2004.

Brill, Marlene Targ. *The Trail of Tears: The Cherokee Journey From Home* (Spotlight on American History). Millbrook Press, 1995.

Fremon, David K. *The Trail of Tears* (American Events). Maxwell Macmillan International, 1994.

Sneve, Virginia Driving Hawk. *The Cherokees* (A First American Book). Holiday House, 1996.

Things to Think About and Do

You Are There

Pretend you are a newspaper reporter in 1838. Write a short newspaper article about General Winfield Scott's U.S. Army troops taking the Cherokees from their homes and putting them in stockades.

Negotiating a Treaty

Imagine that you are one of the Cherokees negotiating the treaty of 1835 that includes the United States' desire to move the Cherokees to Indian Territory (now Oklahoma). Make a list of the arguments you might make for allowing the Cherokees to remain in their homeland in the East.

Starting Over

Imagine that your Cherokee family has just arrived in the wilderness in the West at the end of the Trail of Tears. Write a short essay about all that would have to be done to start life over in that new place.

Setting the Scene

Draw a picture of a Cherokee town complete with homes and farms. Include people in traditional clothing.

A Terrible Journey

Imagine yourself a young Cherokee forced to leave your homeland, and write a day-by-day diary of the Trail of Tears.

Index